Ripe

A Collection of Passionate Poetry and Pears

poems by *Minx Boren*   paintings by *Patti Burris*

To order additional copies of this book, contact:
Xlibris
844-714-8691
www.Xlibris.com
Orders@Xlibris.com

ISBN: Softcover   978-1-4134-7677-4
        Hardcover   978-1-4134-7678-1
        EBook   978-1-6698-4558-4

Library of Congress Control Number: 2004099167

Print information available on the last page

Rev. date: 09/07/2022

On the cover:
"Pearfection"
acrylic on canvas by Patti Burris
© 2004 Patti Burris
all rights reserved

*Dedicated to the Creative Force in each
and every one of us sourcing our infinite capacity
for passionate self-expression.*

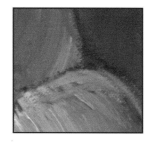

About this book... and our process
Minx

When I wake each morning, I open my eyes to Patti's pears - three paintings that hang on my bedroom wall. They speak to me of passion and pleasure, of connection and mystery, of softness and fullness... all qualities I hope to bring into my day.

I've been writing poems that explore and celebrate passion for many years, hiding them away because they are so raw, so revealing that I never considered sharing them, except with my husband and a few intimate friends. Then, one day, Patti told me about the series of pears she was painting. I decided to ask her to partner with me in creating this book. I sensed that, if my poems could be accompanied by Patti's subtly sensuous art, they would be immeasurably enriched so as to gain a more universal voice.

For these poems are about more, much more, than just my yearnings, my imaginings, and my experiences. Having both befriended and coached countless women (and more than a few brave men), I am well aware of the deep rich vein of passion through which their lifeblood flows. And what I know for sure is that it is well worth the effort it takes to mine it thoroughly, for the yield can be dazzling.

Passion is the underlying force that gives LIFE to life. It awakens the creative seed within our very core (a word derived from the French word "coeur" meaning heart). As poet David Whyte says, "The antidote to exhaustion is not rest. Rather it is wholeheartedness." Passion is the elixir that enlivens us and encourages (another word derived from "coeur") our full self-expression.

Though passion exists on many levels, the poems in this collection are distinctly sensual and sexual. Interestingly, they have bubbled up and out of me only in the years since I turned 50. As I speak with other women who have crossed over that imaginary threshold into middle age (and beyond) I am discovering that they too are having a resurgence of primal yearning, often with no clear sense of how to direct or satisfy this newfound energy. More often than not, there is a reticence to even talk about it. Rather, women seem embarrassed as well as quietly frustrated because their late-life lustiness isn't always shared by the partners in their lives... if there happen to be partners in their lives. My hope is that my poems will spark all sorts of connectivity — starting with rich conversations about needs and desires and pleasuring. Wishful thinking maybe but I have this vision of couples, both young and older, reading my poems to each other... for play.

Whether or not women have significant partners with whom to explore their sexuality is just one of the issues. There is another conversation about passion that needs to be explored. The larger question is how else to harness this energy surging from deep within. Women, young and old alike, are seeking ways to channel their passion. And so I have met women who have taken up painting and women who have taken up political causes. I've connected with women who are sculpting and writing and running marathons and starting businesses or mentoring other younger women who are. All this fiery energy seems to thrive when properly kindled. Perhaps the poems and paintings in this small collection can serve as kindling. THAT would make it well worth the courage I have had to muster to allow you, dear reader, such an intimate glimpse into my soul.

Patti

For several years now, I begin each morning by reading one or two of Minx's poems. It is a practice that both moves and centers me. The poems provide a sense of focus and direction. They resonate within me as self-affirmations that I can carry into my day.

I am sure I was born an artist. Art has always been at the center of my life. When I paint, it is my essence that appears. My brush stroke creates an intimate dialogue as I dance with canvas, palette, and images. This way of being present allows me to connect with an inner rhythm that sustains and guides me.

This series of 85 pear paintings evolved because of my desire to explore new possibilities. As an artist I believe it is important to take risks and stretch beyond the known and familiar. And so I dared myself to create new and untested parameters within which to work. I changed my palette from vibrant hues to rich deep earth tones and reduced the size of my canvases to a consistent 9"x12". I challenged myself to play with the juxtaposition of images and space within these confines. My intention was to create a series where the positive and negative spatial dynamics would dictate the emotion expressed. I did not paint from any prearranged still life. (I did not even consciously choose to paint pears until they appeared on the canvas and I realized how intimately I could identify with their sensuality.) Each painting was birthed from my imagination.

I began slowly and built the series by consciously connecting with my own body language and rhythm. I literally felt each painting as a deep stirring that I could express through my brush and palette. I have enjoyed both the process and the results. This is essential. I tell my students "You own your line." What matters is to be fully involved in the process without worrying about the end results. Ultimately what an artist exposes on the canvas is her own identity and her own way of seeing the world. What I discovered, as I stood before each painting, was the evolution of my own womanliness, my own sensuality… ripe, full, mysterious, wise. Actually, I was surprised and delighted by how sensual the series became. This body of work has evolved into a large wall filled ceiling to floor with these deeply hued paintings hung in close proximity so that they vibrate with one another.

The series has taken almost three years to complete and, toward the end, it was no easy process. Suddenly, in the midst of all the creative exploration, I had to deal with a detached retina in my dominant right eye. After surgery, I could no longer focus the way I used to. There were distortions to which I had to adjust with great patience. I had to rethink my approach to painting. At times I felt sad and afraid, discouraged and frustrated. Unwilling to abandon my lifelong passion for art, I dug deep to find the strength and courage to direct myself and to push my essential voice up and through these new visual restrictions.

What I have learned from all this is to trust and draw upon my inner eye. It took time to once again feel in control of my painting as I found ways to overcome limitations and reach a new place in my art. To refresh my vision, I pause more and enter into intimate dialogues with my paintings. Above all, I am experiencing a fuller, richer, more passionate sense of Self to bring into Life and onto each canvas.

We two women…

… are dear and longtime friends. In the course of conceiving and developing this book together we have both weathered difficult and life-altering challenges. In the process, we have discovered a new expansiveness in our appreciation for LIFE, for our lives, for our creative capacity, for our desire to teach and our passion to learn and explore, and, above all, for the relationships that nurture us. The common thread in our words and images is an ongoing choice to stay fully present and to embrace each moment with hope, resilience, wisdom, passion, and joy.

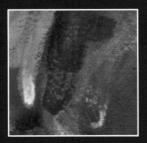

The truly sensuous takes time and a
feeling for the deliberate,
undulating rhythms of the body.

—George Leonard

Contents

soft and juicy 2

it's that man-woman thing 4

exploring your intimate topography 6

there are no words 8

wet wild hungry 10

beloved 12

I remember 14

in the afterglow 16

I will play Calliope 18

rivulets swell into rivers 20

beware the moon 22

I am more 24

ah sweet night 26

familiar rhythms 28

thrown off center 30

love in the morning 32

nude is nicer 34

all this time 36

yet-to-be lovers 38

what if 40

lazing lusciously 42

I can fake it 44

touch me 46

yes 48

frisky pheromones 50

I know you 52

do you ever feel
soft
and juicy

like a luscious fruit
warmed
and ripened
to pearfection
succulent
basking
in your fullness
wanting
to be savored

imagine
how tantalizing and
delicious
to celebrate this
blossoming
allowing your juiciness
to overflow and
anoint your every word
and gesture
to arouse your creative
force
to sweeten each
experience
and enliven
each connection

it's that man-woman thing
you know
you've felt it I'm sure
a thousand times
or once — it does not matter –
that throbbing pulse
deep within
beating out its message
in response
to the beloved
whether across a room or
separated by not so much
as a hair's breadth

it's that "ME Tarzan, YOU Jane" stuff
no kidding
though you've tried I'm sure
a thousand times
or once — it does not matter —
to be reasonable
reason fails unreasonably
when primal longing
screams
to be reckoned with
hungry juicy wild
laughing at the restrictions
of ineffectual niceties

it's got a life of its own
of course
haven't you felt that
a thousand times
or once – it does not matter –
because once aroused
proper containment
within the confines
of propriety and reason
only belies what is so
only squelches the fire
of the furnace
that fuels your creative Self
would you, could you
be so foolish?

it's that do-or-die calling
you've been there
have you not
peering over the edge
a thousand times
or once – it does not matter –
would you, could you
persist in controlling
the uncontrollable
by doling out
carefully measured responses
having even once
unabashedly sampled
the delicious lustiness
of life?

it's that kundalini energy
you've sensed it
in your gut I'm sure
a thousand times
or once – it does not matter –
the snake uncoiling
up and through
the spine of you
sending shivers
inviting you
to shed your skin
to expose your underbelly
and be reborn
to the magnificence
of your passion

can you
    will you
        deny it
            and at what price?

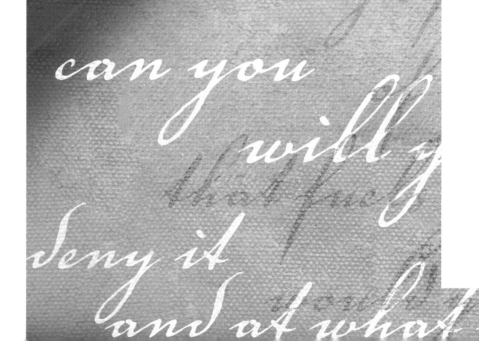

exploring
your intimate topography
with eyes
fingertips
tongue
I lose myself
but not my way
instinctively
propelled forward
by desire

savoring your arousal
I allow my own
full rein
and rise
and rise
to meet the intensity
of your yearning

caressing and clawing
our way to
a rapturous peak
of uncharted territory
we arrive at last
breathless
and grateful
for the adventure

there are no words
only the soft feeling
in my belly
when you rest your head
upon me
only the bold insistent pounding
of my heart
when you are near
only the mounting urgency
arising from my depths
in response to you
caressing me
anywhere and everywhere
only the gasping for breath
all the while knowing
that I am willing to surrender
to the breathlessness of love
only the raw vulnerability
in my eyes
which I shield
from your persistent gaze
only a hunger so deep
that I cannot open myself
enough to receive all of you
and yet there is nothing
I want more
than to try
again and again

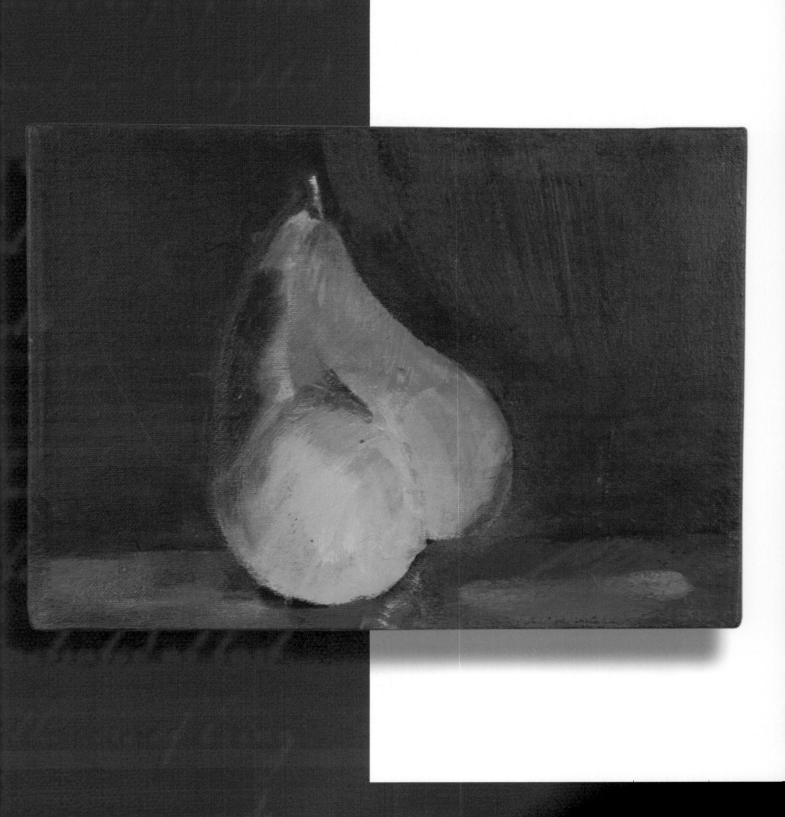

        wet wild

hungry for your taste
aroused to perfection
teased and delighted
by the slightest touch
hot shivers along my spine
anticipating magic

        I wait

flung wide open
a bold pulsing invitation
penetrated at last
to the core of being
there are no words
only sweet abandon

        with such joy

beloved
your arms
are the cocoon
into which
I wish to climb
your neck
the haven
I would choose
to rest
my weary mind
your chest
the place
I want
to press my heart
and let its beat
synchronize to yours
I pray
that as we lie together
time after time
in the sweet surety
of your presence
this deep ache
I carry
will yield
to the power
and fullness
of you

I remember
that first date
a night on the town
pockets emptied
not wanting it to end
we rode around the park
letting a hansom cab
jostle us
into each other's arms

I remember
that first time
a rented room
a bit awkward for sure
like those crazy
love bugs
hanging on for dear life
we tussled
and teased our way
along
smitten yet shy
playing hide and seek
with our emotions

I remember
that first night
on a sandy beach
mosquitoes nipping
at us from behind
and the night on the boat
when the waves
did all the work
and the night we decided
to make a baby
and we did
right then and there
and the night we almost
split
but the lights went out
so we groped
our way back
into each other's arms

all these years later
having almost lost you
the floodgates open
I remember
the sweet journey
of our loving

in the afterglow
the world

my demands
appear less worthy
somehow
of so much
frivolous attention

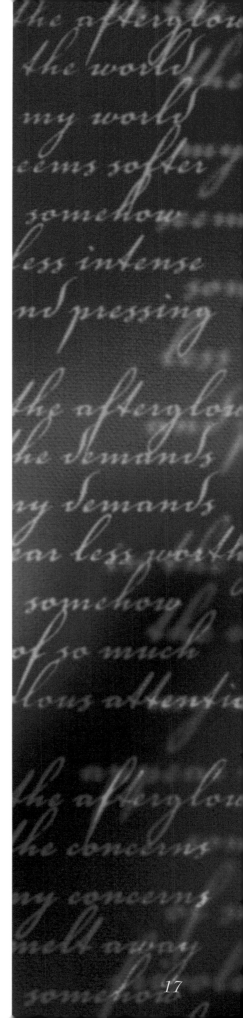

in the afterglow
the world
my world
seems softer
somehow
less intense
and pressing

in the afterglow
the demands
my demands
appear less worthy
somehow
of so much
frivolous attention

in the afterglow
the concerns
my concerns
melt away
somehow
leaving my heart
open and ready
to embrace
everything

I will play Calliope
to your Apollo
I will scribe my passion
heedless of tomorrow
With words will I
arouse your yearning
Scintillating fuel to
stoke your burning
And so your conflagration
will inspire
My poems of lust
love and desire
Warmed by your heat
dazzled by your glow
Ravaged by your flames
my juices will flow
Touched by your brilliance
I will tantalize and amuse
For when passion beckons
who can refuse
Grateful for your warmth
and your light divine
Our stories for eternity
will intertwine

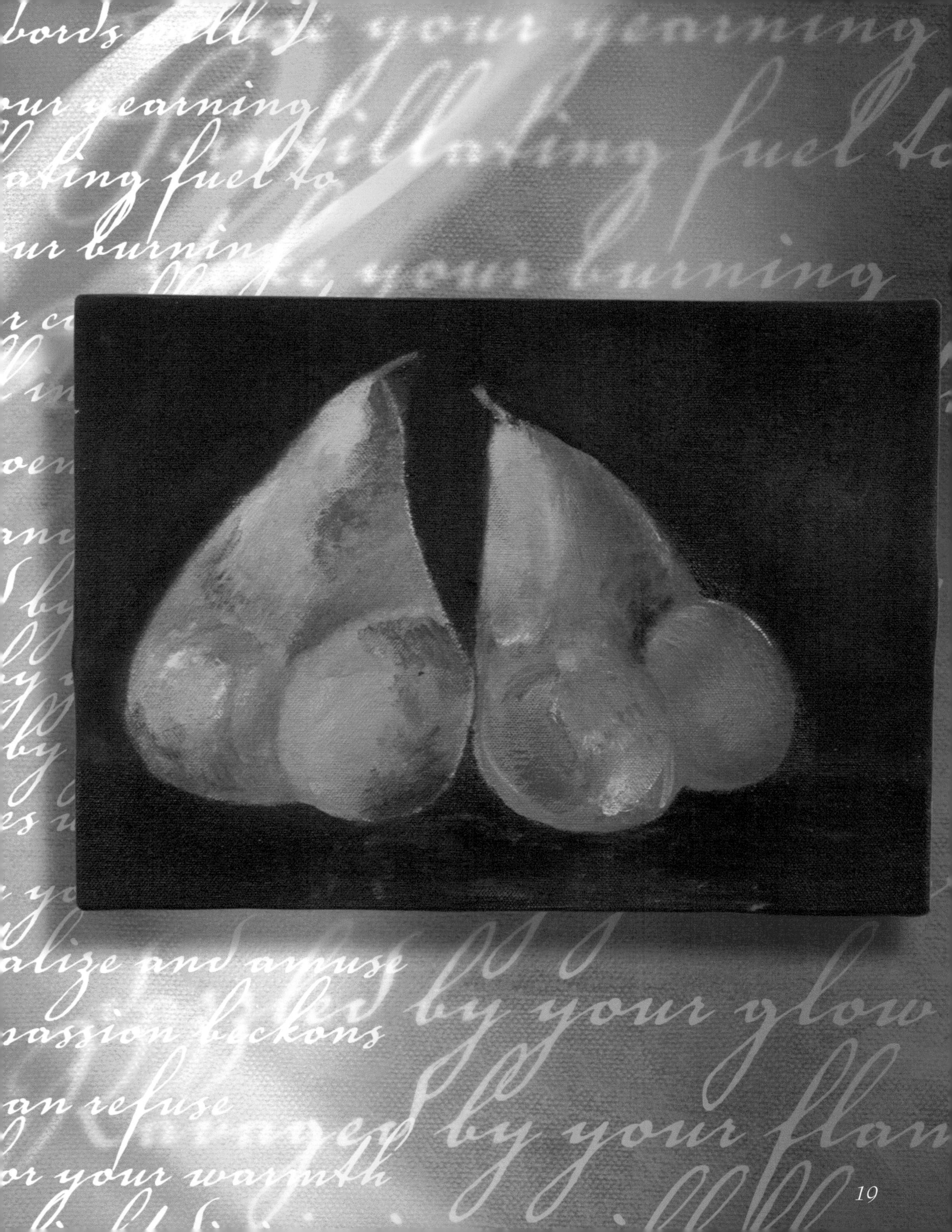

rivulets swell
into rivers
as they make their way
to the sea
tis a journey etched
along her banks
since time before time
a flowing force
shapeshifting
the earth
grain by grain

my heart swells
with joyfulness
as I make my way
to your arms
and press myself against you
leaving an imprint
of my soul upon yours
tis a journey
as ancient as Eden
a magnetic force
shapeshifting
one other
touch by touch

beware

take care

full moon above

crazymaking afoot

we come

undone

it's a puzzlement
the moon
all that subtle force
male and female both
pushing and pulling
at the tides
pulling and pushing
at our hearts
it's a mystery
all that yin-yang energy

curious how
the goddess Diana
a rather independent deity
tends to her silvery orb
all the while
pulling the strings
that make us
mere mortals
dance puppet-like
in her glow

ironic how
the man in the moon
smiles beneficently
a Mona Lisa smile
while we lovers
passion unleashed
emotion unbridled
shift and shimmer
in his light

oh what a night

I am more
so much more
than I have shown you
shyness or reluctance
veil the vastness
of my heart
logic and caution
serve as censors
to the meanderings
of my mind

concealed
is the fullness
of my capacity for joy
hidden
the depth
of my hunger
for connection

my soul dances
at the edge
of your awareness
wanting to expose
her Self
in all her paradoxical splendor
but
I am more
so much more
than you are willing to see

ah sweet night
we two
lovers rest content
on crumpled sheets
exhilarated and fulfilled
surrendering
into the sleepwake space
of these small hours
I feel your heartbreath
and my own
synchronize

you shift and stir
and I find my way
again and again
into the warmth
of your flesh
the curves and angles
of muscle and bone

in this slow
nocturnal dance
I unfold and recurl myself
again and again
while even as you sleep
your lips
find the nape
of my neck
your hands seek
and cradle my breasts
and I am held within

the circle of your love

two lovers
swaying to the rhythm
of the night
moving to some
deep and ancient beat
shapeshifting
to accommodate first one
then the other
entwined in the great comfort
and familiarity of shared love

two lovers
holding fast
to the eternity
of the moment
all the while knowing
that day will soon break
and so will our embrace

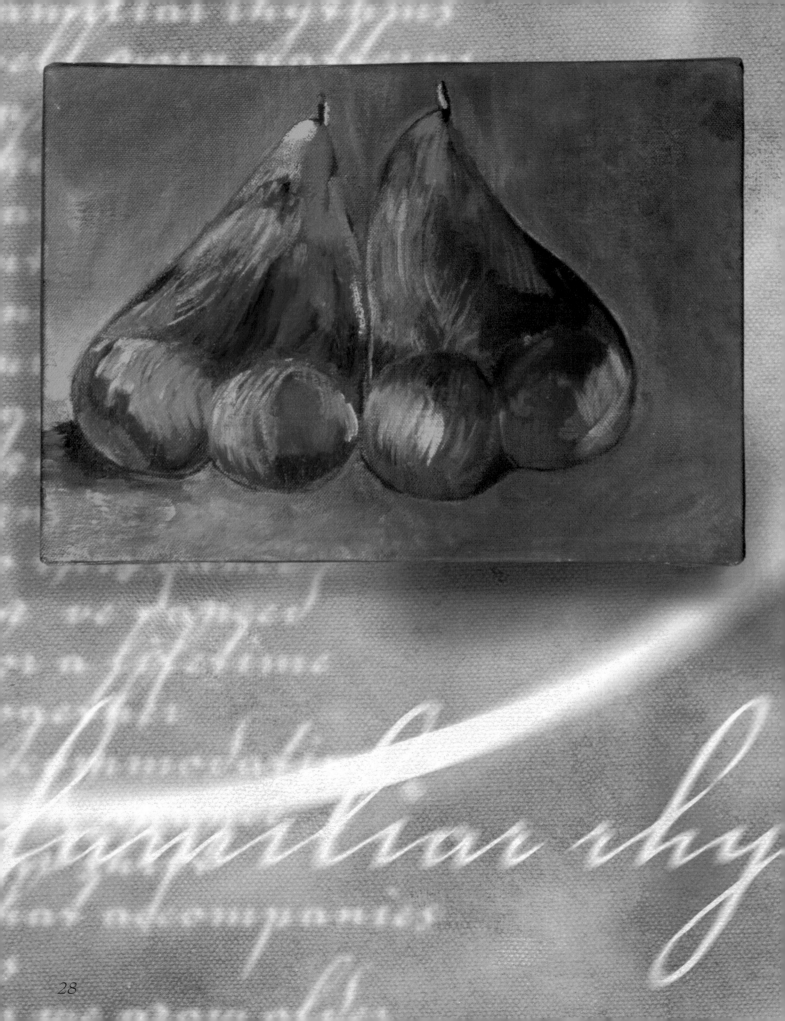

familiar rhythms
well worn patterns
on sheets
that know us
have felt our
intertwinings
and witnessed
our release
again and again
creaky coils
lending music
to this dance
we've danced
for a lifetime
together
accommodating
each nuance
and shift
that accompanies
us
as we grow older
together

thrown off center
by a glance
a knowing look
that pierces
my frivolous façade
how dare you
know me
so intimately
that all the pretense
I can muster
fails to disguise
my yearning
swept away
by a look
like a message
in a bottle
I am left tossing
hither and yon
hoping you will
gather me up
open me
and read my soul

Burns04

31

love in the morning
slow kindling
glowing embers
breathed to life
by patient attention
sleepy reluctance
giving way
to mounting urgency
until a roaring blaze
consumes all

love in the afternoon
playful
giddy and wild
deliciously unpredictable
a spontaneous adventure
inspired by a glance
or a scent
an escape
from the details and dramas
of an otherwise
ordinary day

love in the evening
hot passion
kept alive
through all the wining
and dining
the touching and teasing
a crescendo
of mounting anticipation
uncontainable
the very moment
we find ourselves
alone at last

nude is nicer
you don't agree
veiled hints
excite your imagination
provocative scantiness
arouses your passion

but for me
naked is nicer
a pure offering
unabashedly exposed
trusting the kindness
of your eyes

without pretense
neither fig leaves
nor fans nor feathers
nor diaphanous ploy
separating my raw desire
from your touch

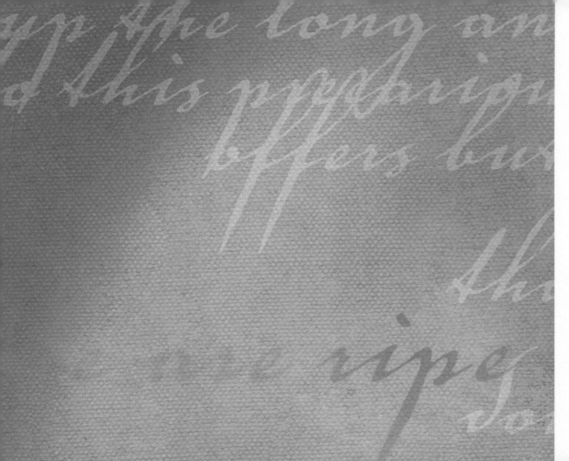

36

all this time
and still
I hunger to discover
whom we might yet become
together
the force of attraction
that has pulled us
up the long and difficult path
to this precarious vantage point
offers but a mere glimpse
of the blessings
that may await us
on the journey
down the other side

we are ripe
and ready
too full and succulent
to remain
on the vine
ready and ripe
to explore
this mysterious passage
this new maturity
if only we will
let go
of the secure hold
of what little we knew
for sure
just yesterday

yet-to-be lovers
daring to touch
newly unsure
of the steps
to a ritual
as old as time
exploring
listening for
finding
their own rhythm
cellular memories
amplified by
quickening pulses

about-to-be lovers
discovering
harmonious movement
born of
deep inner knowing
the dance
once begun
finds its own tempo
self and other joined
whirl around in the moment
coming at last to
a grand finale

two hearts
beat their applause
as now-at-last lovers
bow appreciatively
to one another
and wait expectantly
for the encore

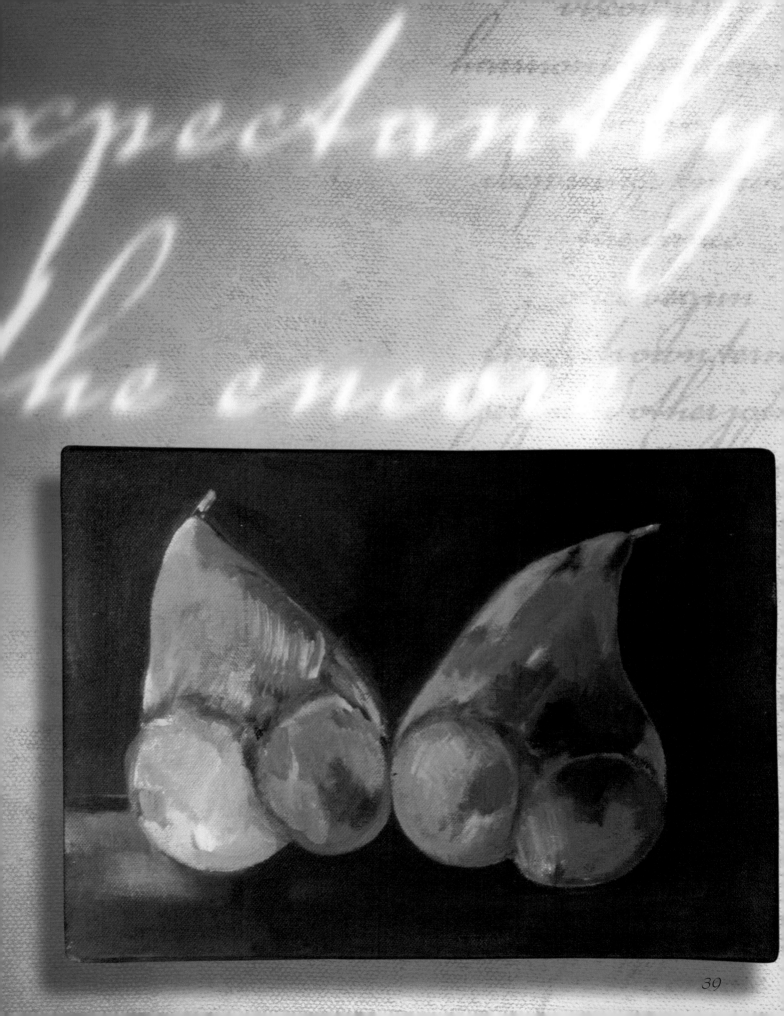

39

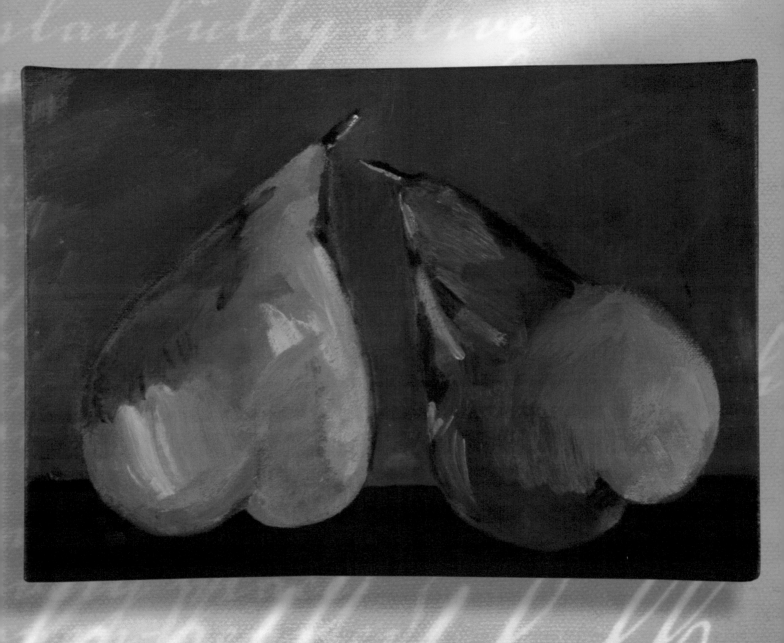

what if
making love
to life
were the one
true way

playfully alive
passionate
joyfully awake
vulnerable
our yearning to reach
out and touch
the Divine
in everyone and everything
overt and bold

smiles as kisses
every place
open-hearted
amazement
seeking the Beloved
everywhere every time

every experience
an electrified
connection
recharging us cell
by cell

every encounter
nourishing us
as we gather and share
love that falls
like manna from heaven

lazing lusciously

on crumpled sheets

bodies entwined

anointed

by the juiciness

of our desire

propelled into spaciousness

by the thrust

of our passion

drifting easily

in time out of time

sweet dreams

my Beloved

sweet dreams

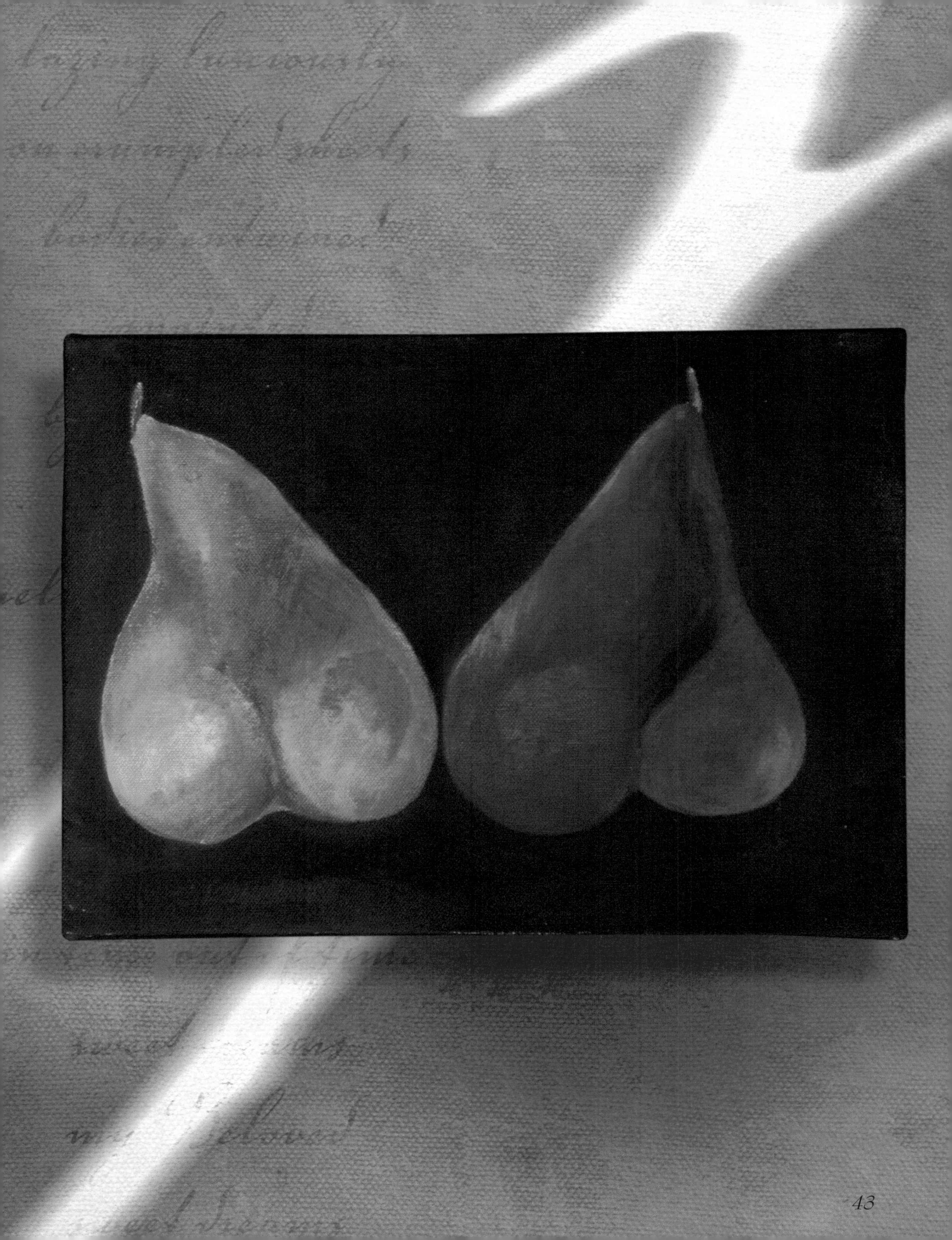

I can fake it
but not force it
I can ride it
but never steer it
I can fight it
struggle
to suppress it
but why would I
when in fact
by losing myself
I win

I can explore it
but never contain it
I can surf
the orgasmic waves
of pleasure
again and again
paddling out to meet
the next great crest
but then I must
surrender my whole self
to its turbulent
and foamy surge

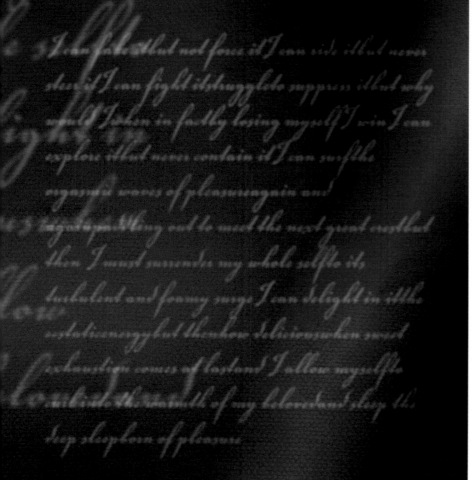

I can delight in it
the ecstatic
energy
but then
how delicious
when sweet exhaustion
comes at last
and I allow myself
to curl into
the warmth of my beloved
and sleep
the deep sleep
born of pleasure

touch me
here and now
by that sweet gesture
bridge my aloneness
all pain soothed
whole self quivering
awakened electrified
by the connection
yet so very at peace

touch me
now and here
celebrate our aliveness
with an embrace
of all the senses
the most precious
the most necessary
you touching me
touching you
bridges everything

sweet gesture bridging aloneness
now by that sweet
gesture bridge my
aloneness all pain
soothed whole self

senses the most

precious the most

necessary you

touching me

touching you

there is so much
embedded
in the word
"yes"
I do
I will
open my mind and heart
inviting another
to see
what lies hidden there

oftimes
we cannot say
why we say
"Yes!"
and "YES!" again
I shall
I must
open my Self
and allow another
to touch
my soul

an irresistible force
like a magnet
somehow attracts
some one
special being
into our life
for a moment in time
or a lifetime
and
with open arms
and heart and soul
there can be
but one response
"YES!"

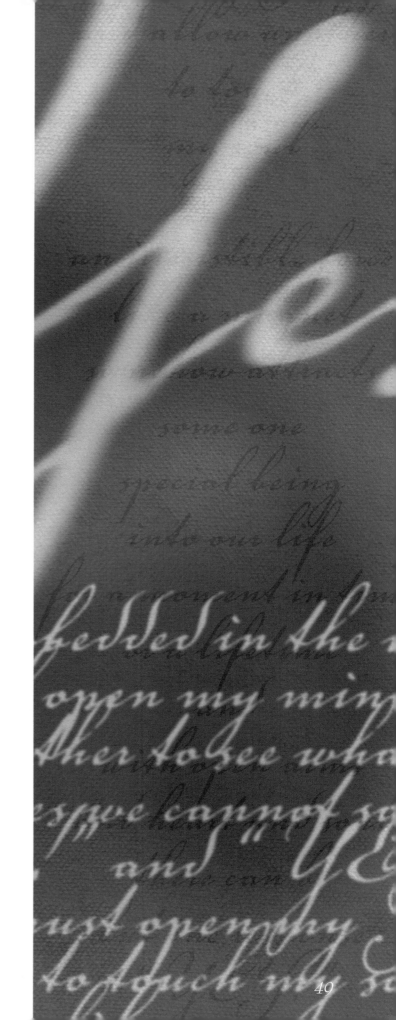

it's not ME
it's those frisky pheromones
playing
seek and collide
on the radar screen
of my senses
all sex
oooooops
six of them

suddenly
I'm all ears
and fingertips
tinglings and titillation
while
my scentsory antennae
pick up
those unmistakable signals
pouring
out of your pores
wafting my way
on the winds
of passion

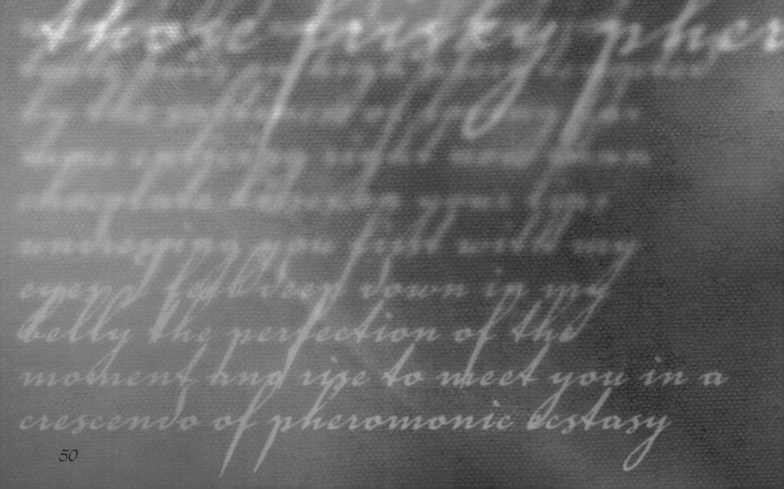

taste buds
on high alert
tempted
by the saltiness
of loving
far more enticing
right now
than chocolate
kisses
on your lips

undressing you
first with my eyes
I feel
deep down
in my belly
the perfection
of the moment
and rise to meet you
in a crescendo
of pheromonic ecstasy

I know you.
Haven't I always known you?
cellular memories
from somewhere
deep inside
push up and through
today's amorphous reality
revealing a primal bond
awakened by your presence

You know me.
Haven't you always known me?
this connection
so deep and familiar
binding us
soul to soul
must have had its birth
in time before time
how magnificent
to have found you again

Thank you, dear reader, for taking the time to be with us, to glimpse the sensual images of our mind's eye made audible and visible. Our deepest wish is to have struck a resonating chord in your being, for then we shall all be blessed.

Namaste

Minx & Patti

P.S. A very last thought. As someone wise once said, "Never underestimate the power of being naked and smiling."

Printed in the United States
by Baker & Taylor Publisher Services